CW00566627

L. T. C. R(

a bibliography

originally compiled by
Ian Rogerson and **Gordon Maxim**
with the assistance of
Sonia Rolt

edited and revised
and with an Introduction by
Mark Baldwin

B

M & M BALDWIN
Cleobury Mortimer, Shropshire
1 9 9 4

First published in 1986
Second edition, revised and extended, 1994

ISBN 0 947712 04 6

Published by M & M Baldwin
24 High Street, Cleobury Mortimer, Kidderminster, Worcs DY14 8BY

Printed by Severnside Printers Ltd
Bridge House, Upton-upon-Severn, Worcs WR8 0GH

1 Tom Rolt at the wheel of his 1924 Alvis, Bryneglwys, 1951

2 The Cressy medallion, 1981

CONTENTS

INTRODUCTION TO THE FIRST EDITION

by Mark Baldwin

When Lionel Thomas Caswall Rolt (always known as 'Tom') was born in 1910, the railway system in the British Isles had been developed almost to its fullest extent, canals were still an important part of the transport scene, steam power was widely used both in stationary and moving machinery, and such cars as did exist were hand-built. For a mechanical engineer, it was in many ways a Golden Age, and one which Tom Rolt admired and loved, even to the extent of describing himself as an 'Edwardian'.

A private tutor laid an excellent educational foundation but, alas, seven years of boarding school failed to build much of substance on this. Rolt left school at sixteen, and was advised by a family friend, Kyrle Willans, to train as a mechanical engineer. He started with Bomfords, farmers of Pitchill, who had a sizeable engineering workshop to care for their steam ploughing engines and other agricultural machinery. Two years later, he was apprenticed to Kerr, Stuart & Co. in Stoke-on-Trent, where he was working on the development of a diesel lorry when the company went bankrupt in 1930. After several more jobs, a love of cars (and a desire for independence) asserted itself and led in 1935 to his establishing with a friend the Phoenix Green Garage at Hartley Wintney, near Basingstoke, to specialise in caring for those vehicles whose high-quality engineering appealed strongly to Rolt. This partnership lasted for four years, during which time Rolt realised that the formation of an enthusiasts' club would help to ensure both the preservation and the enjoyment of well-built cars. Accordingly, the Vintage Sports-Car Club was formed in 1934 with Tom as a founder member.

By the end of 1938, Tom had become disenchanted with the changing nature of cars, particularly when mass-produced, and of their owners. This, and impending marriage to Angela Orred, led to Tom's selling his share of the garage and buying a wooden boat, *Cressy*, to serve as a floating home for him and his wife. Tom had known *Cressy* of old, as she had at one time belonged to Kyrle Willans, who had taken Tom on several cruises. On the very first of these, as Tom later declared, he fell 'head-over-heels in love with canals'. Angela's wealthy father had disapproved of Tom to the extent of cutting his daughter's allowance to a very modest level, so Tom's choice of living afloat had a practical basis; they would be able to live very cheaply while exploring the waterways of England. At the same time, Tom would have the opportunity to pursue his ambition to write, developing a talent of which he had only lately become aware, and to which he wished to give himself more fully.

Their honeymoon cruise began in July 1939 and lasted for several months. The delight it evoked inspired Tom's first book *A Painted Ship* which did the dreary round of publishers in 1940 and 1941, and was eventually consigned to a suitcase under the bed. There it lay until a chance inquiry from H.J. Massingham led to its enthusiastic publication in 1944 by Eyre & Spottiswoode under the title *Narrow Boat*. It has proved to be a compelling book, with a power born from the author's intimate knowledge and love of his subject. Although unforeseen by Rolt, the focus created by the publication of *Narrow Boat* led in 1946 to the formation of the Inland Waterways Association, of which Tom became the first secretary. *Narrow Boat* has triumphed over those faint-hearted and sceptical publishers, not only because it has hardly been out of print for 50 years, but also because it demonstrated to Rolt that his abilities as a writer were in fact substantial.

Despite the early successes of the IWA, 1951 was a year of great personal disaster for Tom; his marriage failed, he was expelled from the IWA following disagreements on policy, and *Cressy* exhibited rot beyond repair. Turning his back on the waterways, Tom found in the Talyllyn Railway a new outlet for his fascination with things mechanical. The Talyllyn was a privately owned narrow-gauge line in central Wales, on the verge of bankruptcy. Tom's vision, and his organising and mechanical abilities, transformed it into a flourishing passenger railway, restored and operated by volunteers. This type of revitalisation had never before been attempted, although it is now widely accepted as a practicable approach for many lines of no interest to a nationalised railway industry.

During this post-waterway period, Tom married again. His second wife was Sonia Smith, one of the 'Idle Women' - a band of girls who had been trained to operate canal boats during the Second World War. Through her work for the IWA, she had become a member of the IWA Council and had thus met Tom. They went to live in the house which Tom's father had bought in Stanley Pontlarge, and this remained Tom's home for the rest of his life. It was here their sons, Tim and Dick, were born and brought up, and where Tom died in the Spring of 1974.

During the last twenty years of his life, Tom emerged as a leading figure in the field of industrial history. His ability and experience were recognised both by his appointment to high office, and by academic honours. He became Vice-President of the Newcomen Society, Chairman of the Council for British Archaeology's Research Council, amongst other appointments, and was instrumental in the establishment of the Railway Museum at York. He received two honorary degrees: Master of Arts at Newcastle University in 1965, and Master of Science at Bath University in 1973.

Tom's whole-hearted dedication to preserving the creations of early engineers, his own engineering training, and his literary ability, put him into a unique position to write engineering history and make it into a subject of interest to a wide readership. He managed, despite very considerable practical involvement with the IWA and the Talyllyn, to write about 50 books, and 250 booklets, articles, book reviews and similar shorter pieces. These cover the whole range of engineering history, from the beginnings of the steam age right through to aviation, motorways and the Severn Bridge. His work shows great diversity of form, including standard technical histories, commissioned company histories, fiction, autobiography, and three brilliant biographies - of Telford, Brunel and the Stephensons - for which he is probably best known. Indeed, no-one since Samuel Smiles has approached engineering history and biography on such a scale, and it is certain that the work he has done has shaped today's attitudes to the artefacts of yesterday's engineers.

* * * * *

Given the extent and importance of Rolt's output, the publication of a bibliography of his work is an obviously significant project although, as so often, it appears obvious only after somebody else has had the initial idea. Full credit for initiation of this work must, therefore, go to Ian Rogerson who, as Gloucestershire's County Technical Librarian, first compiled and published a short list of Rolt's work in 1968. He subsequently became Librarian at Manchester Polytechnic where, with the assistance of Gordon Maxim and Joyce Barlow, he considerably extended and updated the bibliography, listing for the first time many of Rolt's contributions to periodicals. He has generously given permission for his work to form the basis of this present publication. Additional information has been provided by Sonia Rolt, who has also willingly furnished references from the Rolt Collection, and checked successive drafts.

Despite the earnest endeavours of the several contributors, the goal of completeness, which forever tantalises the bibliographer, has not been achieved. We have included everything written by Rolt that we could locate, and also everything written about him with the exception of a few minor newspaper articles. However, the work of as prolific a writer as this is necessarily widely spread, and there are doubtless articles and letters we have failed to discover. Let me end, then, with a plea rather than an apology: the publishers would be most grateful to receive information about items inadvertently omitted from this bibliography. Future editions will thereby form a finer, more complete tribute to Britain's greatest engineering historian.

ACKNOWLEDGEMENTS

In addition to those named in the Introduction, a number of other people have provided assistance, namely Michael Chrimes (Deputy Librarian of the Institution of Civil Engineers), Richard Dalby, Peter Hull (Secretary of the Vintage Sports-Car Club), Robert Humm, E.L. Marshall, Alex McMullen (editor of *Motor Boat & Yachting*), Graham Thorne, and D. Woodhouse (General Manager of the Talyllyn Railway Company). To all these, sincere thanks are extended.

EDITOR'S NOTE ON THIS NEW EDITION

In the first edition of this bibliography, I expressed the hope that a revised and updated edition might be a possibility at some stage. Indeed, as soon as the text of the first edition had been sent to the printer, I started to make notes for just that purpose. The reception given to the first edition fully justified our faith in the book, and I am now delighted to be able to launch a revised and updated edition. It is particularly appropriate that this should appear in 1994, fifty years after the first publication of *Narrow Boat*. Included are 78 new entries, bringing the total to 366, while several dozen of the original entries have been amended to correct or extend them, or to record new editions. The numbers of some new entries will be found to bear suffix letters; these serve no other purpose than to preserve both the correct sequence of entries and the original numbering system.

Above will be found a record of those whose contributions to the text of the first edition were so valuable. For this new edition, thanks are due to all those who produced extra material, in particular to Sonia Rolt for further data from the Rolt Collection, and Gordon Mountford for checking many of the new entries against his own collection. Others who kindly made suggestions for improvements or provided information include: Eric Alston, John Boyes, Joyce Brown, Kay Crooks, Richard Dalby, John Fletcher, Gordon Higlett, Cynthia Hirons, H. Hodgkinson, Clare Humm, Robert Humm, Bill Jenkins, O.H. Prosser, Gerald Quartley, P. Roberts, Christopher Roden, Dr Richard Ross, Matthew Searle, Sandy Skinner, Dr Norman Smith, Ernie Stevens, Reg & Pam Taylor, David Thirlby, Graham Thorne and Gordon Webb.

We are grateful to the Centre for the History of Technology, Science & Society, University of Bath, for locating and permitting the use of photograph no. 23. The print of no.1 was provided by the Rolt Collection, from a photograph by J.B. Snell. Richard C. Packer took nos. 2, 7, 9, 11, 15 and 19. The rest were taken by the editor. Myfanwy Baldwin keyboarded the entire text, no easy task with nearly a thousand font changes.

Mark Baldwin
Cleobury Mortimer
October 1994

BOOKS and BOOKLETS
(Non-fiction)

WATERWAYS

01 **Narrow boat: illustrated by D.J. Watkins-Pitchford, with a foreword by H.J. Massingham.**
London: Eyre & Spottiswoode, 1944. 212pp, illd, map.
The story of a 400-mile voyage in narrow boat *Cressy* through the canals of the Midlands in 1939-40. This seminal work led to the formation of the Inland Waterways Association, and hence to the foundation of the modern canal movement.
2nd imp 1945; revd edn 1948. Reprinted 1957, 1965, 1971, 1972, 1978. Readers' Union edn 1946. Right Book Club edn 1949. Pprbk edns by Eyre Methuen (London) 1978, 1980, 1984.

02 **Inland waterways.**
London: Association for Planning & Regional Reconstruction, 1946. (APRR Report R41). 12pp.

03 **Green and silver, with photographs by Angela Rolt.**
London: Allen & Unwin, 1949. 275pp, illd, maps. Dust-jacket designed by Evelyn Hunt.
An account of a journey on the waterways of Eire in 1946.
2nd imp 1968, with new Foreword. New edn by Athlone Branch of the Inland Waterways Association of Ireland 1993, with new Foreword by Ruth Delany.

04 **The inland waterways of England.**
London: Allen & Unwin, 1950. 221pp, illd, map, bibl. Dust-jacket designed by Barbara Jones.
A full introduction to the history, construction and working of the waterways from the Middle Ages, including the author's appraisal, from personal experience, of the then surviving community of canal boatmen.
Reprinted 1955, 1962, 1966, 1970. 2nd edn 1979, with Foreword by Charles Hadfield. US edn by Kelley (Clifton, New Jersey) 1970.

05 **The Thames from mouth to source, illustrated in colour from old water colours and aquatints, with notes on the artists and illustrations by Francis Maxwell.**
London: Batsford, 1951. x, 86pp, illd, map, bibl.
General account, including personal impressions of a journey in *Cressy* in 1950.

06 **Inland waterways.**
London: Educational Supply Assn, 1958. (Information Book. How Things Developed series). [vi], 90pp, illd, maps.
2nd edn 1961.

07 **Waterway.**
London: Newman Neame, 1961. (Take Home Book series). 15pp, illd.

08 **Look at canals: illustrated by John James.**
London: Hamish Hamilton, 1962. (Look Book series). 91pp, illd, maps.
For children.

09 **Navigable waterways.**
London: Longmans, 1969. (Industrial Archaeology series No 1). xiv, 188pp. illd, maps, bibl.
Rolt was also general editor of the series.
2nd imp 1971. Pprbk edn by Arrow Books (London) 1973. New pprbk edn by Penguin (Harmondsworth) 1985, revd by Bryan Marsh.

10 **From sea to sea: the Canal du Midi.**
London: Allen Lane, 1973, ix, 198pp, illd, maps, bibl.
Describes the history of this 17th-century canal, which inspired the Duke of Bridgewater's canal in the next century.
US edn by Ohio University Press (Athens) 1974.

3 Item 01: *Narrow Boat* (1944)   **4** Item 03: *Green & Silver* (1949)

RAILWAYS

11   **Lines of character . . . in association with P.B. Whitehouse.**
London: Constable, 1952. 188pp, illd, bibl.
An exploration of some byways of the railways of the British Isles.
2nd edn, with new Introduction, subtitled 'a steam age evocation; with photographs by P.B. Whitehouse' by Harvester Press (Hassocks, Sussex) 1974.

12   **Railway adventure: [with a] foreword by John Betjeman, drawings by James Boswell.**
London: Constable, 1953. xiii, 176pp, illd, map.
The story of the Talyllyn Railway in Merioneth and its revival by the Talyllyn Railway Preservation Society in 1950, in which the author played a leading role. The society's success proved for the first time that volunteers could sustain and give new life to the surviving relics of industrial archaeology.
New edn by David & Charles (Dawlish) and Phoenix House (London) 1961.
2nd imp 1977. Country Book Club edn, 1962. Pprbk edn by Pan Books (London) 1971. New edn by Alan Sutton (Gloucester), 1993. (See also Items 21 and 24).

13   **A railway revived.**
Birmingham: Talyllyn Railway Preservation Society, [1955]. 5pp, illd.
Reprinted from *Out of Doors*, March-April 1955. (See also Item 116.)

14   **Red for danger: a history of railway accidents and railway safety precautions.**
London: J. Lane, 1955. [ii], 225pp, illd, bibl.
2nd edn by David & Charles (Newton Abbot), 1966. 2nd imp 1971. US edn by Taplinger (New York) 1967. 3rd edn by David & Charles (Newton Abbot) 1976, updated by G.M. Kichenside. 2nd imp 1978. 4th edn by David & Charles (Newton Abbot) 1982. Pprbk edns/imps by Pan Books (London) 1960, 1966, 1967 (twice), 1971, 1978, 1986.

15   **The Railway Museum, York. The background story of the exhibits.**
London: British Transport Commission, 1958. 23pp, illd.
Reprinted 1962, 1964, 1965, 1968 (revd), 1970, 1971. 3rd and subsequent impressions by British Railways Board.

16   **Railways.**
London: Newman Neame, [1958]. (Take Home Book series). 15pp, illd.

17   **Look at railways; illustrated by Thomas Godfrey.**
London: Hamish Hamilton, 1959. 96pp, illd.
For children.
Reprinted 1960, 1962. School edn 1963 in 'Look Book' series, reprinted 1967. Revd edn, illd by John Young, by Panther (London) 1969 in 'Panther Look Book' series.

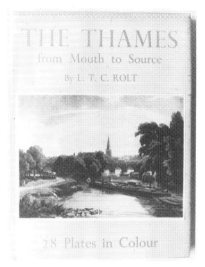

5 Item 05: *The Thames* (1951)   **6** Item 14: *Red for Danger* (1955)

18 **The Great Western Railway Museum, Swindon.**
London: British Railways Board, 1963. 31pp, illd.
An historical guide.
Reprinted 1964, 1966. 2nd edn 1968, reprinted 1971, 1972, 1973

19 **Alec's adventures in railwayland.**
London: Ian Allan/Loco Publishing Co, 1964. 47pp, illd.
A parody, satirising the railway mangement of the Beeching period.

20 **Patrick Stirling's locomotives.**
London: Hamish Hamilton, 1964. (Hamish Hamilton Monograph No 6).
64pp, illd.
An account of the Scottish engineer who brought about the revival of the single-wheeler express locomotive.
Canadian edn by Collins (Don Mills, Ontario) 1964.

21 **Talyllyn century: the Talyllyn Railway 1865-1965. edited by L.T.C. Rolt.**
Dawlish: David & Charles; London: Macdonald, 1965. 123pp, illd, maps.
Compiled to celebrate the centenary of the incorporation of the Talyllyn Railway Company on 5th July 1865. Besides being editor and writing the Introduction, Rolt was one of seven contributors, each of whom wrote one chapter. Companion volume to Item 12. (See also Item 24.)
US edn by Taplinger (New York) 1965.

22 **Railway engineering.**
London: Macmillan, 1968 (Quantum Book series No 9). 112pp, illd.
Aimed at intelligent young readers, this book summarises the technical and social problems faced by modern railways.

23 **The making of a railway: photographed by S.W.A. Newton.**
London: Evelyn, 1971. 2-154pp, illd, maps.
Narrative linking contemporary photographs of the building of the Great Central, 1894-1899.
2nd imp 1979. New edn by Sutton (Gloucester) 1990.

24 **Talyllyn adventure: introduced by L.T.C. Rolt.**
Newton Abbot: David & Charles, 1971. 289pp, illd, maps.
Contains texts of Items 12 and 21.

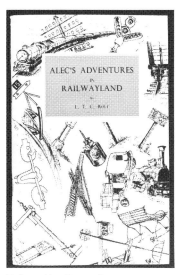

7 Item 19: *Alec's Adventures* (1964)   **8** Item 20: *Patrick Stirling's Locos* (1965)

MOTORING

25 **Horseless carriage: the motor car in England.**
London: Constable, 1950. 204pp illd, bibl. Dust-jacket designed by Barbara Jones.
An outline of the evolution of the motor car in England, in which Continental and Transatlantic influences played a part, and of the progress from craft to mass production methods.
2nd imp 1954.

9 Item 25: *Horseless Carriage* (1950) 10 Item 26: *A Picture History of Motoring* (1956)

26 **A picture history of motoring.**
London: Hulton Press, 1956. (Picture History series). 160pp, illd, map.
Nearly 500 pictures from 1769 to 1955, with linking narrative.
2nd imp 1957. US edns by Macmillan (New York) 1956, and Peebles Press (New York), 1974. The latter is entitled 'Motoring: a pictorial history of the first 150 years' and has an added coloured frontis, and a new Foreword by Rolt.

27 **Motor cars.**
London: Educational Supply Assn, 1957. (Information Book. How Things Developed series). [vi], 104pp, illd.
US edn by Taplinger (New York) 1960.

28 **The motor car: an exhibition of books illustrating the development of the motor car. . . Organised by L.T.C. Rolt.**
London: National Book League, [1958]. 45pp.
Catalogue, with Introduction by Rolt.

29 **Inside a motor car, with drawings by John W. Wood.**
London: Ian Allan, 1964. (Inside Story series No 2). 60pp, illd.
Technical description, for children, of Morris Minor 1000.

30 **Motoring history.**
London: Studio Vista; New York: Dutton, 1964. (Dutton Vista Picture Back series). 159pp, illd.
The history of the automobile from Cugnot's model steam carriage of 1783 to 1963.

OTHER TRANSPORT

31 **Transport treasures: some historical relics of British transport.**
London: British Transport Commission, 1956. 32pp, illd.
Issued in conjunction with an exhibition in the Shareholders' Room at Euston Station, London.
2nd edn 1962.

32 **The London - Birmingham Motorway: South of Luton - Dunchurch - Crick section.**
London: Laing, [c1960]. 64pp, illd.
Booklet commemorating the building of part of the M1, Britain's first major motoway.

33 **The Severn Bridge: the story of its history and construction.**
Gloucester: Gloucestershire County Council, 1966. 70pp, illd, maps.
Commemorative booklet. 2nd imp 1966.

34 **The aeronauts: a history of ballooning, 1783-1903.**
London: Methuen, 1967. 267pp, illd, bibl.
A comprehensive history.
Pprbk edn by Sutton (Gloucester) 1985.

35 **Transport and communications.**
London: Methuen, 1967. (The World We Are Making series). 136pp, illd.
An outline for children, with drawings by Paul Sharp.
2nd edn 1972.

36 **The Tyne Tunnel.**
Newcastle: Tyne Tunnel Joint Committee, 1967. 47pp, illd.
Commemorative booklet.

37 **Mersey Tunnel 2: the story of the second Mersey Tunnel and approach roads.**
[Liverpool: Mersey Tunnel Joint Committee, 1971]. 47pp, illd.
Commemorative booklet.

38   **Holloways of Millbank: the first seventy-five years.**
London: Newman Neame for Holloway, 1958. [vii], 57pp, illd.
Official history of Holloway Brothers (London) Ltd, builders and civil engineers.

39   **Mariners' market: Burnyeat Limited: growth over a century.**
London: Newman Neame for Burnyeat, 1961. [vi], 62pp, illd.
Official history of Liverpool ships' chandlers.

40   **The Dowty story.**
London: Newman Neame for the Dowty Group, 1962. vi, 90pp, illd.
Official history, 1931-1961. (See also Item 48).

41   **Thomas Newcomen: the prehistory of the steam engine.**
Dawlish: David & Charles; London: Macdonald, 1963. 158pp, illd, bibl.
First full account of Newcomen's work and its place in the history of the
development of steam power.
2nd imp 1964. 2nd edn, entitled 'The Steam Engine of Thomas Newcomen', by
Moorland Press (Buxton, Derbys) and Science History Pubns/USA (New York),
incorporating additional material by J.S. Allen, 1977, produced as a memorial
volume under the auspices of the Newcomen Society.

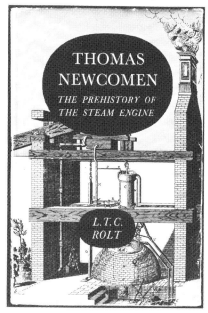 

11 Item 41: *Thomas Newcomen* (1963)   **12** Item 44: *The Mechanicals* (1967)

42   **A Hunslet hundred: one hundred years of locomotive building by the Hunslet Engine Company.**
Dawlish: David & Charles; London: Macdonald, 1964. 177pp, illd.
US edn by Taplinger (New York) 1965.

43   **Tools for the job: a short history of machine tools.**
London: Batsford, 1965. 265pp, illd, bibl.
First comprehensive history of the subject published in England.
US edn by MIT Press (Massachusetts) 1965, entitled 'A short history of machine tools'. Revd pprbk edn by HMSO (for Science Museum), 1986.

44   **The Mechanicals: progress of a profession.**
London: Heinemann for the Institution of Mechanical Engineers, 1967. xii, 163pp, illd.
Official history of the Institution.

45   **Waterloo Ironworks: a history of Taskers of Andover, 1809-1968.**
Newton Abbot: David & Charles, 1969. 3-240pp, illd.
US edn by Kelley (Clifton, New Jersey) 1969.

46   **Golden Jubilee, 1919-1969.**
London: Fedn of Civil Engineering Contractors. 1969. 15pp, illd.

46B   **The Tasker Museum of Rural Engineering.**
Andover, Hants: TM Trust, [c1970]. [12]pp, illd.
'Text prepared by L.T.C. Rolt'.

46D   **Lansing Bagnall: the first 21 years at Basingstoke.**
Basingstoke: for the company, 1970. x, 63pp, illd.
Fork-lift truck manufacturers.

47   **Victorian engineering.**
London: Allen Lane, 1970. 300pp, illd.
Pprbk edn by Penguin (Harmondsworth) 1974, reprinted 1977.
Japanese translation published by Kajima Institute Publishing Co Ltd, 1989.

48   **Dowty story, part II, 1961-71.**
London: Cooper, 1973. [v], 64pp, illd.
Second volume of official history. (See also Item 40.)

49   **The potters' field: a history of the South Devon ball clay industry.**
Newton Abbot: David & Charles, 1974. 159pp. illd, bibl.
A full account of this essential, but previously unrecorded, aspect in the development of the making of pottery and porcelain.

13 Item 45: *Waterloo Ironworks* (1969)

14 Item 47: The Japanese edition of *Victorian Engineering* (1989)

BIOGRAPHY

(see also Item 41.)

50 **Isambard Kingdom Brunel: a biography.**
London: Longmans, 1957. xv, 345pp, illd, bibl.
The definitive biography.
Reprinted 1958, 1959, 1964, 1970, 1971, 1972. RU edn 1959. Book Club Assoc
edn 1971. US edn by St Martin's Press (New York) 1959. Pprbk edns by Arrow
(London) 1961, and Penguin (Harmondsworth) 1970 (reprinted several times). The
Penguin edns have no subtitle.

50B **I.K. Brunel.**
Middlesex County Council, [1958]. [i], 13.
Text of first Brunel Lecture, given at Brunel College of Technology, on 22 Jan
1958.

51 **Thomas Telford.**
London: Longmans, 1958. xv, 211pp, illd, bibl.
The definitive biography.
Reprinted 1959, 1962, 1969. Scientific Book Club edn (unilld) 1959. Pprbk edn
by Penguin (Harmonsworth) 1979, later reprinted several times.

52 **The Cornish giant: the story of Richard Trevithick, father of the steam
locomotive.**
London: Lutterworth Press, 1960. 160pp, illd.
US edn by St Martin's Press (New York) 1962.

53 **George and Robert Stephenson: the railway revolution.**
London: Longmans, 1960. xix, 356pp, illd, bibl.
The definitive biography.
4th imp 1971. US edn by St Martin's Press (New York) 1962, entitled 'The railway revolution'. Pprbk edn by Penguin (Harmondsworth) 1978, later reprinted several times.

54 **Great engineers.**
London: Bell, 1962. xii, 244pp, illd, bibl.
Biographies of ten 'great but less famous' engineers. Baker, Crompton, Darby, Fowler, Jessop, Lanchester, Locke, Maudslay, Murray, and Newcomen.
2nd imp 1966. US edn by St Martin's Press (New York) 1963.

55 **James Watt.**
London: Batsford, 1962. 144pp, illd, bibl.
US edn by Arco (New York) 1963.

56 **The story of Brunel, illustrated by Paul Sharp.**
London: Methuen, 1965. (Story Biography series). 118pp, illd.
Biography of I.K. Brunel for younger readers.
US edn by Abelard-Schuman (New York) 1968.

15 Item 50: *Brunel* (1957)

16 Item 51: *Telford* (1958)

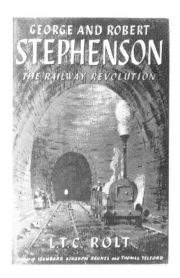

17 Item 53: *The Stephensons* (1960)

18 Item 57: *Worcestershire* (1949)

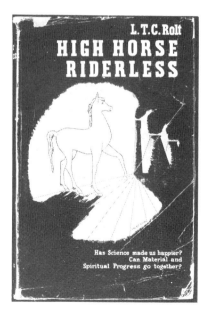

19 Item 58: *High Horse Riderless* (1947)

20 Item 59: *The Clouded Mirror* (1955)

TOPOGRAPHY

57 **Worcestershire.**
London: Hale, 1949. (County Books series). xvi, 295pp, illd, map, bibl.
The first part describes the contribution which generations have made to their native shire. The second part is a portrait of the county in the present century.

57B **The Cottage, Stanley Pontlarge.**
For the author, [c1950]. [4]pp.
Brief history of 'one of the oldest *small* inhabited houses in England'.

PHILOSOPHY and AUTOBIOGRAPHY

Note: several other of Rolt's books contain much autobiographical material, e.g. Items, 01, 03, 05, 12, 21, and 24.

58 **High horse riderless.**
London: Allen & Unwin, 1947. 171pp, illd. Dust-jacket designed by Toni del Renzio.
Individual skill and responsibility contrasted with the centralisation and mass-production of the modern world.
Danish edn: Stolten ganger uden rytter. Paa dansk ved Niels Haislund. Kobenhavn, 1948. Unilld pprbk edn by Green Books (Bideford) 1988.

59 **The clouded mirror.**
London: J. Lane, 1955. 126pp.
Four essays contrasting the life of modern man living under the twin threats of nuclear annihilation and totalitarianism, with that of the individual craftsman and his contribution to the partnership between man and nature. The last essay develops this theme in relation to the metaphysical poets of the Welsh border, who seek in their lives and work to heal the breach between the temporal and the eternal.

60 **Landscape with machines: an autobiography.**
London: Longmans, 1971. xi, 230pp, illd.
Describes his early life, up to 1939.
2nd imp 1971. Pprbk edn by Sutton (Gloucester) 1984. New issue 1994.

61 Landscape with canals, being the second volume of *Landscape with Machines*, an autobiography.
London: Allen Lane, 1977. 188pp, illd, maps.

Starting in 1939, this describes his life aboard *Cressy*, his founding of and subsequent work for the Inland Waterways Association, and his first marriage (to Angela). All three came to an end abruptly in 1951.
2nd imp 1978. Pprbk edn by Sutton (Gloucester) 1984. New issue 1994.

61B Landscape with figures: the final part of his autobiography.
Gloucester: Alan Sutton, 1992. x, 246pp, illd.

Pprbk issue, uniform with preceding two books, 1994.

INTRODUCTIONS and CONTRIBUTIONS

(See also Items 21 and 28.)

62 MASSINGHAM, H.J. (ed). **The small farmer: a survey by various hands.** London: Collins, 1947.

Chapter VI, 'Small machines for small farmers' (pp 229-56) by L.T.C. Rolt.

63 BLAKESTON, Oswell (ed). **Holidays and happy days.** London: Phoenix House, 1949.

One chapter, 'Sailing across England: a holiday on the canals' (pp 33-48) by L.T.C. Rolt, recounts a 400-mile waterway trip in 1947

64 **[Brochure for the Canal Cruising Company.]** Stone: CCC, c1950.

Foreword by Rolt.

65 SINCLAIR, R. et al. **A company's story in its setting: Samuel Williams & Sons Ltd, 1855 - 1955.** London: Williams, 1955.

Rolt contributed pp 41-79, describing the history of this engineering, shipbuilding, lighterage and transport company.

66 GIESL-GIESLINGEN, A. **The first "Giesl ejector" front end in Great Britain.** [?]: Talyllyn Railway Co., 1958.

Introduction by Rolt, pp 3-4.

67   PAINE, E.M.S. **The two James's and the two Stephensons, or The earliest history of passenger transit on railways, by E.M.S.P. A centenary reprint, with introduction by L.T.C. Rolt.** Dawlish: David & Charles; London: Phoenix House, 1961.

67B   WEBBER, J. (selector). **Adventure by road and rail.** London: Hamilton, 1962.
      One chapter, 'The Tay Bridge disaster' (pp 62-71), reprinted from 'Red for danger' (Item 14).

68   INSTITUTION OF MECHANICAL ENGINEERS. **Engineering heritage: highlights from the history of mechanical engineering. Vol 1.** London: Heinemann for IME, 1963.
      Contributions by Rolt: Thomas Newcomen - father of the steam engine (pp 52-6); The Stephensons - A vital partnership (pp 75-9); The younger Brunel: trailblazer and perfectionist (pp 139-44). Reprinted 1964 (twice), 1967, 1969.

68B   MORGAN, Bryan. **The railway lover's companion.** London: Eyre & Spottiswoode, 1963.
      Includes various extracts from 'Lines of character' (Item 11), 'Red for danger' (Item 14), and 'Isambard Kingdom Brunel' (Item 50).

68D   SIMMONS, Jack (ed). **Industrial archaeology: a guide to the technological revolution of Britain.** London: BBC, 1965.
      Rolt contributed 'Transport' (pp 13-16) to this booklet accompanying a television series.

68F   RUSSELL, J H. **Painted engines.** London: Allen & Unwin, 1965.
      One-page Foreword by Rolt.

68H   WHITEHOUSE, P.B. (compiler). **Railway anthology.** London: Ian Allan, 1965.
      Pp 66-70 comprise a reprint of Item 118D.

68J   TALYLLYN RAILWAY PRESERVATION SOC. **Talyllyn Railway Centenary Magazine.** D&C, 1965.
      Rolt contributed 'Steam through 100 years', page 1, and possibly other items.

69   WILKINSON, Tim. **Hold on a minute.** London: Allen & Unwin, 1965.
      Rolt wrote a one-page Foreword to this account of narrow-boat carrying in the late 1940s.
      2nd edn 1970. Pprbk issue by Waterway Productions (Burton) 1977. New edn by Baldwin (Cleobury Mortimer) 1990, with additional Foreword by Sonia Rolt.

HILL, P. & JOHNSON, N. The vintage Alvis. London: Macdonald, 1967.
Extracts from the article 'Alvis Christmases' (Item 142) appear on pp 85, 116-17.

71 SMILES, Samuel. **Industrial biography: ironworkers and tool-makers. A reprint of the 1863 edition with additional illustrations and a new introduction by L.T.C. Rolt.** Newton Abbot: David & Charles, 1967.
Published both in hdbk and pprbk.

71B BLISHEN, Edward (ed). **Miscellany Four.** OUP, 1967.
Rolt contributed 'The Great Atlantic Race', pp 128-34.

72 DRIVE PUBLICATIONS (pub). **Treasures of Britain, and treasures of Ireland.** London: for the Automobile Assn, 1968.
Rolt is credited with an unidentified 'major contribution'. Reprinted several times.

72B SMILES, Samuel. **Lives of the engineers with an account of their principal works . . .** Newton Abbot: David & Charles, 1968. 3 vols.
Facsimile of original edn of 1862, with Introduction by Rolt.

72D TOWYN PUBLICITY BUREAU & THE TALYLLYN RAILWAY CO. (pub). **The official guide to Towyn (Merioneth) and the Talyllyn Railway.** Towyn: TPB & TRC, nd [c1968].
Rolt contributed 'A message from the chairman of the Talyllyn Railway Company' and possibly some of the other material on the railway, which comprises about one third of this 96-page booklet.

73 THURSTON, E Temple. **The "Flower of Gloster", with an introduction by L.T.C. Rolt.** Newton Abbot: David & Charles, 1968.
Facsimile reprint of account of a narrow-boat cruise first published in 1911. Reprinted 1972, both hdbk and pprbk.

74 INSTITUTION OF CIVIL ENGINEERS (pub). **The Institution of Civil Engineers: Great George Street, London SW1. 150th anniversary celebrations, 15-17 July 1968.** London: ICE, [1968].
To this commemorative booklet, Rolt contributed '150 Years' (pp 8-10).

74B CHRISTIE'S (pub). **Catalogue of the Taskers Collection of traction engines . . .** London: Christie's, 1969.
Auction catalogue, with Introduction by Rolt, pp 6-8.

74D EPSLEY, J.G. & YOUNG, W.E.D. **The Thames & Severn Canal.** Corsham: Gazebo, 1969.
Foreword by Rolt.

24

74F MACDONALD, Alec. **Worcestershire in English history.** Wakefield: SR Publishers, 1969, 2nd imp of 2nd edn (of 1944).

> With 2-page Foreword by Rolt (to this imp only).

75 CALDON CANAL SOCIETY. **The Caldon Canal.** Leek: CCS, [c1969].

> Cruising guide, with one-page Foreword by Rolt.
> At least one 'much revised edn' by [c1983].

75B CLEMENTS, Paul. **Marc Isambard Brunel.** London: Longmans, 1970.

> With 2-page Foreword by Rolt.

76 SHELL **Guide to England.** London: Shell-Mex & BP, 1970.

> Rolt wrote 'The industrial heritage' (pp 61-6).

77 BRUNEL, Isambard. **The life of Isambard Kingdom Brunel, civil engineer (1870).** Newton Abbot: David & Charles, 1971.

> Facsimile reprint of original edn of 1870, with Introduction by Rolt.

77B **Encyclopaedia Britannica.** 14th edn, 1973 printing.

> Rolt contributed articles on Brunel and Telford.

THE GREAT MASTERS

Thomas Newcomen - Father of the Steam Engine

by L. T. C. Rolt*

That no portrait exists of him is typical of the obscurity that veils Newcomen's personality. Of all the engineers who have been featured in this series, his is the most elusive figure. But that he was indeed a great master we know from his achievement. In 1963 the Institution and the Newcomen Society for the study of the history of engineering jointly celebrated the tercentenary of Newcomen's birth.

21 Article title from Item 68, *Engineering Heritage*

Readers News

22 Item 106: *Readers News*, April 1946

78 BRACEGIRDLE, B. **The archaeology of the industrial revolution.** London: Heinemann, 1973.
Chapter 2, 'Inland waterways', pp 10-40, by Rolt.

78B RANSOM, P.J.G. **Railways revived: an account of preserved steam railways.** London: Faber, 1973.
With 2-page Foreword by Rolt.

78D **New Encyclopaedia Britannica.** 15th edn, 1974.
Rolt contributed Micropaedia article 'Richard Trevithick'.

79 DE BONO, Edward (ed). **Eureka! How and when the greatest inventions were made.** London: Thames & Hudson, 1974.
Contribtions by Rolt: 'Canal lock' (p 21), 'Railways/railroads' (pp 25-6), 'Steam engine' (p 71), 'Steam turbine' (p 77). These articles originally appeared in *The Sunday Times Magazine* (see Item 178).
2nd imp 1976. Pprbk edn 1979. US pprbk edn by Holt, Rinehart & Winston (New York) 1979.

80 FLETCHER, Harry. **A life on the Humber: keeling to shipbuilding: with an introduction by L.T.C. Rolt.** London: Faber & Faber, 1975.
Also contains an Appendix by Rolt: 'Yorkshire keel canals and river navigations'.

81 DORMAN, Colin Creswell. **The London & North Western Railway.** London: Priory Press, 1975.
This book is dedicated to the memory of Rolt, who died shortly after writing the Foreword.

83 HADFIELD, John. **The best of The Saturday Book.** London: Hutchinson, 1981.
Rolt contributed 'Down on the farm' pp 189-94 (reprint of Item 177).

85 JENNINGS, Paul (ed). **My favourite railway stories.** London: Lutterworth Press, 1982.
Pp 32-7 'The Abbots Ripton disaster', an extract from 'Red for danger' (Item 14).

87 SIMMONS, Jack (compiler). **Railways: an anthology.** London: Collins, 1991.
Contains extracts from Item 12 'Railway adventure (pp 59-60) and Item 14 'Red for danger' (pp 86-7).

PERIODICAL CONTRIBUTIONS
(Non-fiction)

Under each heading, these are listed alphabetically by the title of the periodical (or its issuing body) or book. Book Reviews and Published Correspondence are not classified by subject.

WATERWAYS

101   By waterway to Wales.
Country Life. 21 Nov 1947. pp 1020-2.
Hurleston to Llangollen.

102   The Stratford-on-Avon Canal restored.
Country Life. 9 July 1964. pp 86-8.

102B Countrygoing by waterway.
MOORE, Cyril (ed). **Countrygoing: The fourth Countrygoer book.**
1945. pp 54-6.

102D [Title unknown.]
Everybody's Weekly. 19 Mar 1949.

103   The future of the canals.
The Field. 10 June 1944. pp 604-6.

104   Forgotten waterways:
Motor Boat & Yachting. Aug 1942. pp216-7.

105   Adventure on the Stratford Canal.
Motor Boat & Yachting. July 1947. pp 272-5

106   The chronicle of the 'Cressy'
Readers News. Vol 8(11). April 1946. pp 1-4.
To introduce the RU edn of 'Narrow Boat' (see Item 01).

107   Canal crusade: an extract from 'Landscape With Canals' in which the author describes a difficult voyage up the Welsh Canal in 1947.
Waterways World. Vol 6(7). July 1977. pp 32-4.
See Item 61.

World Digest. April 1945. pp 41-3.

RAILWAYS

109 Saved from the axe.
Argus [House magazine of Charles Churchill Ltd]. No 23. pp 29-31.
The Talyllyn Railway.

109B The guard with a rose: happy memories of the Slow, Mouldy and Jolting Line.
Birmingham Mail. 3 Feb 1950.
Lamenting closure of branch lines.

110 100 years of a Welsh hill railway.
Country Life. 24 June 1965. pp 1586-7.
The history of the Talyllyn Railway.

111 The new railway museum at Towyn.
Country Life. 25 May 1967. pp 1310-1.

112 Engineer extraordinary [I.K. Brunel].
Good Work. Autumn 1966. Vol 29(4). pp 101-5.

112B David Curwen.
The History of Model and Miniature Railways. [date unknown].

113 The great engineer - Isambard Kingdom Brunel.
[American] Horizon (Magazine of the Arts). Vol 1(3). Jan 1959. pp 32-43.

114 Goodbye Puffing Billy.
[American] Horizon (Magazine of the Arts). Vol 6(4). Autumn 1964. pp 72-7.

115 The Talyllyn Railway.
Newcomen Society Transactions. Vol 33. 1960/1. pp 17-29.

116 A railway revived.
Out of Doors. March-April 1955.
See Item 13.

117   A new light on I.K. Brunel.
Journal of the Railway & Canal Historical Society. In two parts: Vol 3(3).
May 1957. pp 42-5. and Vol 3(4). July 1957. pp 62-6.
Copyright summary of an address by Rolt to the Society.

117B Centenary of the Royal Albert Bridge at Saltash.
Railway Magazine. Vol 105(5). May 1959. pp 307-13.

117D The Talyllyn Railway 1950-60.
Railway World. Vol 21(239). April 1960. pp 103-6.

118   A railway in miniature.
The Saturday Book No 20. 1960. pp 221-35.
The Talyllyn Railway. With photographs by Edwin Smith.

118B Isambard Kingdom Brunel.
The Somerset Countryman. Vol 19(12). Jan-Mar 1960. pp 314-17.

118D Farewell to Steam.
The Somerset Countryman. Vol 20(2). Oct-Dec 1960. pp 10-13.

119   York Railway Museum.
Steam Alive. Part 6. 1971. pp 4-9.

120   Engineering report.
Talyllyn News. No 2. Nov 1953. pp 6-7.

121   An old link re-established.
Talyllyn News. No 17. Dec 1957. p 2.
The link is between the Talyllyn Railway Co. and the McConnell family.

122   The Giesl ejector.
Talyllyn News. No 20. Sep 1958. pp 3-4.
Experiment with an Austrian blast pipe and chimney on a Talyllyn loco.

123   Where are we going?
Talyllyn News. No 23. Sep 1959. pp 1-2.
Reflections on changes being made in the Talyllyn Railway during restoration.

124   Some notes on Talyllyn locomotives.
Talyllyn News. No 24. May 1960. pp 1-5.

125   The first ten years.
Talyllyn News. No 27. Sep 1960. pp 1-2.
History of the Talyllyn Railway Preservation Society.

126   Obituary for Forrest Lycett.
Talyllyn News. No 30. July 1961. p 7.

127   Obituary for Lord Northesk.
Talyllyn News. No 40. Dec 1963. pp 1-2.

128   Those routine jobs.
Talyllyn News. No 40. Dec 1963. p 3.

129   Heading for a century.
Talyllyn News. No 41. Mar 1964. pp 2-3.
1965 was the centenary of the Talyllyn Railway

130   The Narrow Gauge Railway Museum Trust.
Talyllyn News. No 49. Mar 1966. pp 12-13.

131   An appreciation of Edward Thomas on his retirement.
Talyllyn News. No 53. Mar 1967. p5.

132   Railway politics.
Talyllyn News. No 54. June 1967. pp 2-3.
Defence of Talyllyn Railway administration.

133   Pat Whitehouse
Talyllyn News. No 54. June 1967. p 6.
Amplification of minutes of Talyllyn Railway Preservation Society's AGM of September 1966.

134   Do it yourself.
Talyllyn News. No 55. Sep 1967 pp 1-2.
Importance of skilled volunteers on the Talyllyn Railway.

135   George Tibbitts.
Talyllyn News. No 60. Dec 1968. p 18.
Obituary

136   R.E.L. Pennoyer.
Talyllyn News. No 61. Mar 1969. p 19.
Obituary

137 Edward Thomas.
Talyllyn News. No 74. June 1972. pp 2-3.

138 The Tallyllyn Railway.
Time & Tide. Vol 31(43). 28 Oct 1950. pp 1081-2 .

139 Railway adventure.
Time & Tide. Vol 33(32). 9 Aug 1952. pp 904-5.
The Talyllyn Railway.

139B Man who spanned the Tamar.
The Times. 2 May 1959. p 7.
Commemorating centenary of Brunel's bridge at Saltash.

140 Reminiscences of a locomotive works.
Trains Annual. 1968. pp 5-11.
Kerr Stuart works at Stoke-on-Trent.

140B Appeal for an old lady.
Vintage Sports-Car Club Bulletin. No 56. Autumn 1957. pp 33-4.
Appeal for funds for restoration of the Talyllyn locomotive 'Dolgoch'.

141 Rescue of a railway.
Wide World Magazine. No 694. April/May 1956. pp 26-7.
The Tallylln Railway.

MOTORING

142 Alvis Christmases.
Bulletin of the Alvis Register. No 67. Dec 1962. pp 2-5.
Christmas memories associated with various Alvis cars. Extracts later reprinted
in Item 70.

143 A March of hares.
Bulletin of the Alvis Register. No 95. Dec 1969. pp 5-6.
Weekend meeting of members of the Alvis Register, with their cars.

144 The ethics of the quality car.
Motor Sport. March 1945. pp 45-7.

144B Cars for connoisseurs.
The Saturday Book No 13. 1953. pp 294-308.

145　The Sunday Times outline history of the motor car.
The Sunday Times. 19 Oct 1958. p 30.
Pictorial history, 'prepared in association with L.T.C. Rolt'.

146　G.N. memories.
Vintage Sports-Car Club Bulletin. No 42. Spring 1954. pp 5-8.
Memories of the author's two G.N. cars.

147　Anglo-American Vintage Car Rally.
Vintage Sports-Car Club Bulletin. No 44. Autumn 1954. pp 5-13.
1954 rally.

147B　The Type 666 Funkwagen.
Vintage Sports-Car Club Bulletin. No 47. Summer 1947. pp 22-4.
Humorous article.

148　Vintage diesel.
Vintage Sports-Car Club Bulletin. No 53. Winter 1956-7. pp 33-7.
Experiments in developing a diesel lorry.

149　Horseless carriageway.
Vintage Sports-Car Club Bulletin. No 64. Autumn 1959. pp 42-8.
Building of southern section of M1.

150　Top secret.
Vintage Sports-Car Club Bulletin. No 77. Spring 1963. pp 18-20.
Satirical article about modern engineering design.

150B　The Talyllyn Railway Centenary Rally 1965.
Vintage Sports-Car Club Bulletin. No 84. Winter 1964. p 20.

151　Vintage Prescott, 1938-68.
Vintage Sports-Car Club Bulletin. No 100. Winter 1968. pp 7-12.
History of track at Prescott.

INDUSTRIAL HISTORY

152　Tools for the job.
Argus [House magazine of Charles Churchill & Co Ltd]. No 27. pp 28-9.
An introduction to the author's book of the same title (see Item 43).

153 Science run mad.
The Aryan Path. Mar 1956. pp 111-15.

154 In the steps of Samuel Smiles.
The Author. Vol 81. Winter 1970. pp 151-5.
Useful brief account of Rolt's literary career.

155 Machines that made the world turn.
Birmingham Post. 27 Jan 1968.
Surviving examples of work of Midland engineers of Industrial Revolution.

156 Cheddleton flint grinding mill.
Birmingham Post. 23 Mar 1968.

157 A collected edition of sermons in iron.
Birmingham Post. 23 Mar 1968.
Preservation of Britain's industrial monuments.

158 The world's first bridge of iron.
Birmingham Post. 6 April 1968,
At Ironbridge.

159 A living monument: sewage pumping station, Leicester.
Birmingham Post. 20 April 1968.

160 Living monuments: Brindley's Dove Aqueduct, Burton.
Birmingham Post. 4 May 1968.

161 Midland monuments: Longden Aqueduct.
Birmingham Post. 18 May 1968.

162 Midland monuments: Forge Mill, Redditch.
Birmingham Post. 1 June 1968.

163 Midland monuments: Sarehole Mill.
Birmingham Post. 15 June 1968.

164 Midland monuments: Trench Inclined Plane.
Birmingham Post. 29 June 1968.

165 Midland monuments. Galton Bridge, Smethwick.
Birmingham Post. 20 July 1968.

166 Industrial monuments: Beam blowing engines, Lilleshall.
Birmingham Post. 3 Aug 1968.

167 Industrial monuments: Bratch Locks, Wolverhampton.
Birmingham Post. 17 Aug 1968.

168 Industrial monuments: Jones' Maltings, Shrewsbury.
Birmingham Post. 31 Aug 1968.

169 Industrial monuments: Dudley Canal Tunnel.
Birmingham Post. 14 Sep 1968.

170 Industrial monuments: sermons in iron.
British Industry. 28 Oct 1966. pp 18-19

171 Monuments of the cast-iron age: a threat to relics of the Industrial Revolution.
Country Life. 4 April 1963. pp 720-1.

23 Tom Rolt signs the register at the degree ceremony at Bath University, 1973

172   Saving the "Great Britain".
Country Life. 23 April 1970. pp 910-2.
Recovery of Brunel's historic steam ship.

173   Thomas Newcomen. The birth of the steam engine.
The Engineer. May 1963. pp 850-3.

174   Spanning history.
Geographical Magazine. Vol 34. Jan 1962. pp 489-501.
Road and rail bridges in Britain.

175   The development of machine tools.
History Today. Vol 21(5). May 1971. 322-8.

176   The history of the history of engineering.
Newcomen Society Transactions. Vol 42, 1969/70. pp 149-58.
The 9th Dickinson Biennial Memorial Lecture.
First issued as an undated separate preprint, paginated 1-10.

176B Down in the dark: a subterrestrial excursion.
The Saturday Book No 14. 1954. pp 121-33.

176D The swan song of steam.
The Saturday Book No 15. 1955. pp 264-75
Excludes railway locos. Illustrations provided by Ronald H. Clark.

176F Engineering as an art.
The Saturday Book No 17. 1957. pp 197-206.

177   Down on the farm.
The Saturday Book No 30. 1970. pp 50-7.
Steam traction on the farm. With drawings by Leslie Thompson.
Reprinted in 'The best of The Saturday Book' (Item 83).

178   Eureka: the Sunday Times history of inventions.
The Sunday Times Magazine. Various dates during 1970. Rolt contributed
'The canal lock' (21 June, p 32); 'Steam engine' (5 July, p 26); 'Railways'
(19 July, pp 16-17); 'Steam turbine' (2 Aug, p 24).
Later reprinted in Item 79.

179   A carpenter's shop.
Time & Tide. Vol 37(19). 12 May 1956. p 548.
The decline of the self-employed tradesman.

180 Skill of the 'Stonehenge' foundrymen is still one of the objects of modern admiration.
The Times. 31 March 1973. p IV of Special Report 'The Dawn of Industry' to mark opening of Ironbridge Gorge Museum, 1 April 1973.

OTHER SUBJECTS

181 Mass entertainment.
The Field. 17 Mar 1945.

182 Is mechanisation a menace?
The Field. 25 Aug 1945.
Author given as 'L.T.C. Holt'.

183 "Output per man" on the farm.
The Field. 1 Sep 1945.

183B The passing of the ghost story.
Ghosts & Scholars. No 11, 1989. pp 27-31.

184 Makers and money-men.
Good Work. Spring 1960. Vol 29(2). pp 60-4.
Extract from 'The clouded mirror' (Item 59).

185 Imagination and the dramatic art.
Kingdom Come. Summer 1941. Vol 2(4). pp 113-14.

185B The passing of the ghost story.
The Saturday Book No 16. 1956. pp 105-12.
Later reprinted as Item 183B.

186 The Englishman's castle.
Time & Tide. Vol 38(32). 10 Aug 1957. pp 982-3.

187 The Weekly Competition.
Time & Tide. Vol 40(13). 28 Mar 1959. p 365.
Rolt set this, and reported on the results in Vol 40(17) 25 April 1959. p 477.

188 Lilies that fester.
Time & Tide. Vol 40(15). 11 April 1959. p 410.
Carmelite Educational Trust buy out tenant famer near Cheltenham. See also Items 272 and 273.

189 Letter to a surrealist.
Voices. Autumn 1946. pp 65-70.

BOOK REVIEWS
(all subjects)

190 A review of philosophy. [Book reviewed: E.A. Burtt. **In search of philosophic understanding.**]
The Aryan Path. Oct 1967. pp 470-1.

191 The nature of Man. [Book reviewed: J. Lewis and B. Towers. **Naked ape or homo sapiens?**]
The Aryan Path. Nov 1969. pp 500-2.

191B Rural lines. [Book reviewed: Eric S Tonks. **The ironstone railways and tramways of the Midlands.**]
Birmingham Post. 24 March 1959.

192 Practical peer. [Book reviewed: H. Malet. **The Canal Duke.**]
Birmingham Post. 20 June 1961.

193 Telford's triumphs in the Highlands. [Book reviewed: A.R.B. Haldane. **New ways through the Glens.**]
Country Life. 17 May 1962. p 1203.

194 Industrial monuments [Book reviewed: Kenneth Hudson. **Industrial archaeology: an introduction.**]
Country Life. 7 Nov 1963. p 1190.

195 Wealden waterways. [Book reviewed: P.A.L. Vine. **London's lost route to the sea.**]
Country Life. 3 June 1965. p 1356.

196   Unsatanic mills. [Book reviewed: Kenneth Hudson. **The industrial archaeology of Southern England.**]
Country Life. 4 Nov 1965. p 1197.

197   Dreamland next stop. [Book reviewed: H.A. Vallance (ed). **The railway enthusiast's bedside book.**]
Country Life. 19 May 1966. p 1258.

198   Britain's legacy of canals. [Books reviewed: Charles Hadfield. **The canals of the East Midlands.** and **The canals of the West Midlands.**]
Country Life. 9 June 1966. p 1469.

199   Those magnificent men. [Book reviewed: Charles Gibbs-Smith. **The invention of the aeroplane.**]
Country Life. 9 June 1966. p 1469.

200   Victorian giants. [Books reviewed: E.G. Barnes. **The rise of the Midland Railway.** and F.A.S. Brown. **Great Northern locomotive engineers.**]
Country Life. July 1966. p 162.

201   Chocolate and cream. [Book reviewed: Michael Harris. **Great Western coaches. 1890-1954.**]
Country Life. 25 Aug 1966. p 456.

202   The life and death of an Irish railway. [Book reviewed: Patrick J. Flanagan. **The Cavan and Leitrim Railway.**]
Country Life. 14 Nov 1966. p 1394.

202B   Rural tramways. [Book reviewed: Bertram Baxter. **Stone blocks and iron rails.**]
Country Life. 16 Feb 1967. p 357.

202D   The atmospheric caper. [Book reviewed: Charles Hadfield. **Atmospheric railways.**]
Country Life. 15 June 1967. p 1536.

202F   The golden age of railways. [Book reviewed: P.C. Allen & A.B. Macleod. **Rails in the Isle of Wight.**]
Country Life. 29 June 1967. p 1671.

203   Sagas of steam. [Books reviewed: O.S. Nock. **British steam locomotives at work.** and **The GWR Stars, Castles and Kings, Part 1: 1906-1930.**]
Country Life. 7 Sep 1967. p 532.

204   The story of the Great Central. [Book reviewed: W.A. Tuplin. **Great Central Steam.**]
Country Life. 5 Oct 1967. p 825.

205   Railway over Mendip. [Book reviewed: Robin Atthill. **The Somerset and Dorset Railway.**]
Country Life. 7 Dec 1967. p 1534.

206   Western waterways. [Book reviewed: Charles Hadfield. **The canals of South West England.**]
Country Life. 14 Dec 1967. p 1606.

207   Waterloo empire. [Book reviewed: R.A. Williams. **The London and South Western Railway: the formative years.**]
Country Life. 9 May 1968. p 1220.

208   Royal railway. [Book reviewed: A.D. Farr. **The Royal Deeside line.**]
Country Life. 31 Oct 1968. p 1129.

209   Romance on the rails. [Book reviewed: Hamilton Ellis. **The engines that passed.**]
Country Life. 27 Feb 1969. p 471.

210   Steaming in the 20th century. [Book reviewed: W.A. Tuplin. **British Steam since 1900.**]
Country Life. 20 Mar 1969. p 661.

211   Men of Steam. [Book reviewed: O.S. Nock. **Steam locomotive.** (2nd edn.)]
Country Life. 3 Apr 1969. p 825.

212   Cruising with a purpose. [Book reviewed: David Owen. **Water rallies.**]
Country Life. 1 May 1969. p 1110.

213   Lines of the Lanky. [Book reviewed: John Marshall. **The Lancashire and Yorkshire Railway. Vol 1.**]
Country Life. 8 May 1969. p 1176.

214   Unconquered Steam. [Book reviewed: Gerald Nabarro. **Steam nostalgia.**]
Country Life. 28 Sep 1972. p 727.

215 Through the carriage window. [Book reviewed: E. Churton. **The railroad book of England.**]
Country Life. 25 Oct 1973. p 1281.

216 The industrial past. [Books reviewed: various.]
The Countryman. Autumn 1968. pp 159-61.

217 The industrial past. [Books reviewed: various.]
The Countryman. Spring 1969. pp 150-1.

218 Enticements to exploration. [Books reviewed: various.]
The Countryman. Summer 1969. pp 349-51.

219 Books ancient and modern. [Books reviewed: various.]
The Countryman. Spring 1970. pp 146-8.

220 Rough seas, still waters. [Books reviewed: various.]
The Countryman. Summer 1970. pp 353-5.

221 Infinite riches. [Books reviewed: various.]
The Countryman. Winter 1970. pp 368-71.

222 Orkney to the Scillies. [Book reviewed: various.]
The Countryman. Summer 1971. pp 157-9.

223 Relics of regional life. [Books reviewed: various.]
The Countryman. Autumn 1971. pp 163-4.

224 All our yesterdays. [Books reviewed: various.]
The Countryman. Winter 1971. pp 170-1.

225 Providing the setting. [Books reviewed: various.]
The Countryman. Winter 1972. pp 165-6.

226 [Book reviewed: H. McKnight. **Canal and river craft in pictures.**]
Inland Waterways Association Bulletin. No 91. Jan 1970. pp 83-4.

226B [Book reviewed: H.J. Dyos & D.H. Aldcroft. **British transport: an economic survey from the seventeenth century to the twentieth.**]
Nature. Vol 224, 13 Dec 1969. p 1131.

226D Steam power at sea. [Book reviewed: H. Philip Spratt. **The birth of the steamboat.**]
New Scientist. Vol 5. 23 Apr 1959. p 925.

227 [Book reviewed: Charles Hadfield. **The canals of South Wales and the Border.**]
Journal of the Railway & Canal Historical Society. Vol 6(6). Nov 1960. pp 117-18.

228 [Book reviewed: H.W. Dickinson. **A short history of the steam engine.**]
Technology & Culture. Vol 6(1) 1965. pp 115-8.

229 [Book reviewed: T.P. Hughes (ed). **Lives of the engineers: selections from Samuel Smiles.**]
Technology & Culture. Vol 8(1). 1967. pp 97-9.

230 [Book reviewed: D.B. Barton. **The Cornish beam engine.**]
Technology & Culture. Vol 9(3). 1968. pp 492-4.

231 [Book reviewed: F. Nixon. **Industrial archaeology of Derbyshire.**]
Technology & Culture. Vol 11(3). pp 475-7.

232 [Books reviewed: D. Morgan Rees. **Mines, mills and furnaces: industrial archaeology in Wales.** R.A. Buchanan & Neil Cossons. **The industrial archaeology of the Bristol region.** R.A. Buchanan. **The industrial archaeology of Bath.**]
Technology & Culture. Vol 11(4). 1970. pp 633-5.

233 [Book reviewed: D. Kennedy. **The birth and death of a Highland railway.**]
Technology & Culture. Vol 13(1). 1972. pp 77-8.

234 [Book reviewed: D. Alderson. **Bicycling, a history.**]
Technology & Culture. Vol 14(4). 1973. pp 644-5.

235 [Book reviewed: O. Skeat. **George Stephenson, the engineer and his letters.**]
Technology & Culture. Vol 15(4). 1974. pp 639-41.

236 Showboaters. [Book reviewed: Philip Graham. **Showboats: the history of an American institution.**]
Time & Tide. Vol 33(12). 22 Mar 1952. pp 283-4.

237 England's food. [Book reviewed: H.J. Massingham and Edward Hyams. **Prophecy of famine.**]
Time & Tide. Vol 35(47). 20 Nov 1954. pp 1551-2.

238 Battles long ago. [Book reviewed: Hamilton Ellis. **British railway history, 1830-1876.**]
Time & Tide. Vol 35(47). 20 Nov 1954. pp 1551-2.

239 Muck without mysticism. [Book reviewed: J.C. Wylie. **Fertility from town wastes.**]
Time & Tide. Vol 36(10). 5 Mar 1955. pp 304-5.

240 The guarded mount. [Book reviewed: Sidney Toy. **A history of fortification from 3110 BC to AD 1710.**]
Time & Tide. Vol 36(37). 10 Sep 1955. p 1176.

241 Continental cuts. [Book reviewed: Roger Pilkington. **Small boat through Belgium.**]
Time & Tide. Vol 38(39). 28 Sep 1957. pp 1201-2.

242 The motor moguls. [Books reviewed: Roger Burlinghame. **Henry Ford.** Saint Loup. **Renault.**]
Time & Tide. Vol 39(5). 1 Feb 1958. pp 137-8.

243 Speed kills. [Book reviewed: Roger Pilkington. **Small boat through Holland.**]
Time & Tide. Vol 40(8). 21 Feb 1959. p 220.

244 Historic currents. [Book reviewed: Robert Brittain. **Rivers and Man.**]
Time & Tide. Vol 40(17). 25 April 1959. pp 478-9.

245 A half-told tale. [Book reviewed: Robert Payne. **The canal builders.**]
Time & Tide. Vol 40(42). 17 Oct 1959. pp 1135-6.

246 Scandinavian sortie. [Book reviewed: Roger Pilkington. **Small boat to the Skagerrak.**]
Time & Tide. Vol 41(18). 30 Apr 1960. p 488.

247 [Book reviewed: D.Tew. **The Oakham Canal.**]
Transport History. Vol 1(3). 1968. pp 293-4.

248 [Book reviewed: C.T.G. Boucher. **James Brindley, engineer, 1716-1772.**]
Transport History. Vol 2(2). 1969. p 202.

249 [Book reviewed: J. Thomas. **Gretna, Britain's worst railway disaster (1915).**]
Transport History. Vol 3(1). 1970. pp 108-9.

250 [Book reviewed: M.A. Kelly. **The overtype steam road waggon.**]
Transport History. Vol 4(3). 1971. pp 305-6.

251 [Book reviewed: R. Barker and A. Harding (eds). **Automobile design: great designers and their work.**]
Transport History. Vol 5(1). 1972. pp 97-8.

252 [Book reviewed: K.R. Day. **The Alvis car, 1920-1966.**]
Vintage Sports-Car Club Bulletin. No 91. Autumn 1966. p 26.

253 [Book reviewed: Peter Hull and Norman Johnson. **The vintage Alvis.**]
Vintage Sports-Car Club Bulletin. No 94. Summer 1967. pp 44-5.

PUBLISHED CORRESPONDENCE
(all subjects)

254 21st anniversary of the register.
Bulletin of the Alvis Register. No 94. Sep 1969. p 14.

254B The Talyllyn Railway.
Birmingham Post. 14 Sep 1949.
A slightly different version of this letter was included on pp 29-30 of WHITEHOUSE, P.B. 'On the narrow gauge.' (Nelson, 1964).

254D The Royal Oak.
Country Life. 4 Jan 1946.

255 Timber supplies and the craftsman.
Country Life. 22 Mar 1946. p 540.
Rolt was one of four signatories.

256 Canals and inland waterways.
Dock & Harbour Authority. Vol 30. Feb 1950. p 303
Reply to an article by Sir H. Osborne Mance: 'Suggested outline for a canal transport policy' in *Dock & Harbour Authority.* Vol 30. Jan 1950. pp 265-8.

? ?? Farming and nostalgia,
The Field. 6 Jan 1945.

258 Britain's part in the industrial revolution.
Industrial Archaeology. Vol 5(1). 1968. pp 94-5.
Reply to an article by M. Rix in *Industrial Archaeology.* Vol 4(2). 1967.

258B Industrial archaeology.
The Listener. Vol 74. 18 Nov 1965. p 803.

259 L&NWR road services.
Journal of the Railway & Canal Historical Society. Vol 9(3). May 1963.
pp 44-5.

259B [Untitled letter about the problem of frost in steam cars].
Steam Car Developments & Steam Aviation. June 1934. pp 19-20.
Earliest Rolt publication yet located.

Sir,

I was very interested in your leaflet concerning your proposed revival
of "Steam Car Developments." Please put me down as a subscriber.

I am afraid my experience of steam cars is very limited, but as a
possible line for discussion, I should like to raise the question of frost.

This problem occurred to me when examining the Doble cars at the
Sentinel Waggon Works in December last, it being extremely cold at

24 Opening sentences of Item 259B, the earliest known Rolt publication (1934)

259D [Untitled letter suggesting that a steam car should be entered for the
Shelsley Walsh Hill Climb].
Steam Car Developments & Steam Aviation. Sep 1934. pp 77-8.
Reprinted in *The Magazine of the Malaysia and Singapore Vintage Car Register.*
Mar/April 1994. pp 105-6.

260 Locomotives.
Talyllyn News. No 27. Sep 1960. pp 21-2.
Amplifies the article on Talyllyn locomotives in *Talyllyn News.* No 25. May 1960
(see Item 124) and replies to critics.

261 Flanges of driving wheels on locomotive 'Talyllyn'.
Talyllyn News. No 39. Sep 1963. pp 10-12.

262 Locomotive design.
       Talyllyn News. No 60. Dec 1968. pp 50-1.

263 The threat to Wales.
       Time & Tide. Vol 31(1). 7 Jan 1950. pp12-13.

264 Education of canal boat children.
       Time & Tide. Vol 31(16). 22 Apr 1950. p 394.

265 Pity the author.
       Time & Tide. Vol 34(12). 21 Mar 1953. pp 364-5.
       Effect of income tax on writers.

266 Belloc's world and ours.
       Time & Tide. Vol 34(33). 15 Aug 1953. p 1071.

267 Can we save Democracy?
       Time & Tide. Vol 34(47). 21 Nov 1953. p 1513.
       Proposes formation of an Anti-Bureaucratic League.

268 Can we save Democracy?
       Time & Tide. Vol 34(50). 12 Dec 1953. p 1647.

269 Isambard Kingdom Brunel.
       Time & Tide. Vol 35(44). 30 Oct 1954. p 1445.
       Asking for material for the biography he was writing.

270 Citizen and state.
       Time & Tide. Vol 35(49). 4 Dec 1954. p 1610.

271 The case of the locked lock.
       Time & Tide. Vol 36(22). 28 May 1955. p 708.

272 Lilies that fester.
       Time & Tide. Vol 40(17). 25 April 1959. p 472.
       See also Items 188 and 273.

273 Lilies that fester.
       Time & Tide. Vol 40(19). 24 May 1959. p 524.
       See also Items 188 and 272.

274 Craftsmen in wood.
       The Times. 28 Feb 1946. p 5.
       Rolt was one of four signatories.

275   Rail and canal rates
      The Times. 16 Jan 1950. p 5.

276   Talyllyn Railway.
      The Times. 20 Feb 1951. p 5.

277   National Park control.
      The Times. 22 Jan 1972. p 13.

278   Keeping the railways going.
      The Times. 3 Sep 1973. p 13.

279   The first piston engine.
      Vintage Sports-Car Club Bulletin. No 77. Spring 1963. p 26.
      Appeal for funds for preservation of Newcomen engine from Hawkesbury
      Junction, Coventry Canal.

281   A dastardly affair.
      Vintage Sports-Car Club Bulletin. No 81. Spring 1964. p 36.
      On Formula 1 racing car design. Signed 'Thomas Caswall'.

25 Item 276: From *The Times,* 20 Feb 1951

26 Item 401: *Sleep No More* (1948)

FICTION

390 The cat returns.
Mystery Stories. c1937.
Later reprinted in 'Sleep no more' (Item 401).

395 New corner.
Mystery Stories. c1937.
Later reprinted in 'Sleep no more' (Item 401).

401 **Sleep no more. Twelve stories of the supernatural.**
London: Constable, 1948. vii, 162pp.
2nd edn by Harvester Press (Hassocks, Sussex) 1974, under new subtitle: 'railway, canal and other stories of the supernatural'.

402 **Winterstoke.**
London: Constable, 1954. 248pp, maps.
The story of an imaginary Midlands town from its beginning until the 1950s. It describes the surge of resource and invention, which led to the development of the early iron industry, and the economic and social problems which this left in its wake.

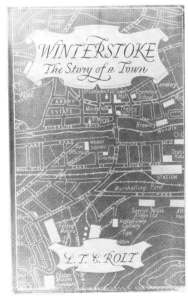

27 Item 402: *Winterstoke* (1954)

28 Item 403: *Best Railway Stories* (1969)

402B 'The mine' *in* Edmund CRISPIN (ed). **Best talon of terror.** London: Faber & Faber, 1962.

A short story, pp 45-51, first published in 'Sleep no more' (Item 401).

403 **Best railway stories: edited with an introduction by L.T.C. Rolt.** London: Faber, 1969. 256pp.

Also includes Rolt's 'The Garside Fell disaster', pp 139-48, from 'Sleep no more' (Item 401).

403B 'Hawley Bank Foundry' *in* Hugh LAMB (ed). **A wave of fear.** London: Allen, 1973.

A short story, pp 80-101, first published in 'Sleep no more' (Item 401). Pprbk edn by Coronet, 1976.

404 'The shouting' *in* Hugh LAMB (ed). **The thrill of horror.** London: Allen, 1975.

A short story, pp 78-83.

404B 'The Garside Fell disaster' *in* Bryan MORGAN (ed), **Crime on the lines: an anthology of mystery short stories with a railway setting.** London: Routledge & Kegan Paul, 1975.

Pp 166-73, first published in 'Sleep no more' (Item 401).

405 'The house of vengeance' *in* Hugh LAMB (ed). **The taste of fear.** London: Allen, 1976.

A short story, pp 186-97. Pprbk edn by Coronet, 1977.

407 'The mine' *in* Jack SULLIVAN (ed). **Lost souls: a collection of English ghost stories.** Ohio Univ. Press, 1983.

Pp 324-9, first published in 'Sleep no more' (Item 401).

409 'Bosworth summit pound' *in* Michael COX & R.A. GILBERT (eds). **The Oxford Book of English ghost stories.** London: OUP, 1986.

First published in 'Sleep no more' (Item 401). Spanish edn 'Historias de fantasmas de la literatura inglesa'. Vol II. Barcelona: Edhasa, 1989, with 'La esclusa cumbre de Bosworth', pp 290-301.

411 'New corner' *in* R. DALBY & R. PARDOE (eds). **Ghosts & scholars: ghost stories in the tradition of M.R. James.** London: Crucible, 1987.

First published in *Mystery Stories*, c1937 (Item 395). Pprbk edn by Equation, 1987.

413 'The mine'
Alfred Hitchcock's Mystery Magazine. 32(12), Dec 1987. pp 141-6.

A short story, first published in 'Sleep no more' (Item 401).

415 'The Garside Fell disaster' *in* R. DALBY (ed). **The mammoth book of ghost stories.** London: Robinson, 1990.
Pp 505-12, first published in 'Sleep no more' (Item 401).

417 **Two ghost stories.**
Chester: BC Enterprises, 1994. v, 16pp, illd.
'The shouting' and 'The house of vengeance'.

BIOGRAPHICAL MATERIAL BY OTHERS
(listed chronologically and excluding reviews of Rolt's books)

501 This month's author [i.e. author of this month's 'Book of the Month'].
Readers News. Vol 8(12). May 1946.

502 Wedged under bridge.
Birmingham Mail. 20 May 1947.

503 "Test" barge passes bridge - with an effort.
Birmingham Gazette. 21 May 1947.

504 WATERS, Brian. The "Cressy" at Sharpness.
Gloucestershire Countryside. Summer 1948.

505 Seeking pleasure on canals.
Yorkshire Post. 1 Sep 1948.

506 Banbury canal boat forms writer's permanent home.
Banbury Advertiser. 17 Nov 1948.

506B THOMAS, Gilbert. Machine madness.
Christian World. 27 Oct 1955. p 4.
Commentary on Rolt's philosophy

507 DARKLR, Ronald. The silent giants of Cornwall.
Autocar. Vol 116(3523). 23 Aug 1963. pp 318-21. and Vol 116(3524). 30
Aug 1963. pp 380-2.
A car trip with Max Millar and Tom Rolt to visit stationary steam engines.

508 ROGERSON, Ian. **L.T.C. Rolt: books and monographs.**
Cheltenham: Gloucestershire Technical Information Service, 1968. 18pp.

508B **L.T.C. Rolt. Engineer, historian, author.**
Derbys County Liby, [c1970]. [9]pp repro from TS.

509 BUCHANAN, R.A.   Mr L.T.C. Rolt.
The Times. 14 May 1974. p 18.
Obituary.

509B BUCHANAN, Angus.   [Obituary.]
Industrial Archaeology. 11(2). p 77.

510 HADFIELD, Charles.   L.T.C. Rolt.
Waterways World. June 1974. p 29.
Obituary.

511 BUCHANAN, R.A.   L.T.C. Rolt, first President of the AIA.
AIA Bulletin. No 1.2. 1974. p 1.
Obituary.

511B 'C.C.' [i.e. Cecil CLUTTON].   L.T.C. Rolt: an obituary.
Vintage Sports-Car Club Bulletin. No 122. Summer 1974. pp 7-8.

512 STEVENS, Philip A.   L.T.C. Rolt, 1910-1974.
Journal of the Railway & Canal Historical Society. Vol 20(2). July 1974.
p 56.
Obituary.

512B 'W.B.'   L.T.C. Rolt - an obituary.
Motor Sport. July 1974.

513 HADFIELD, Charles, and MUNK, Lionel.   The late Mr. L.T.C. (Tom)
Rolt - tributes: IWA's first Secretary.
Inland Waterways Association Bulletin. No 110. Sep 1974. pp 6-7.

514 BUCHANAN, R.A.   Tom Rolt.
CME (The Chartered Mechanial Engineer). Vol 21(11). Dec 1974.
pp 49, 74.
Obituary.

515 'A.W.S.' [i.e. A.W. SKEMPTON].   Lionel Thomas Caswall Rolt.
MA, MSc, FRSL.
Newcomen Society Transactions. Vol 46. 1973-4. p 93.
Obituary.

516 BUCHANAN, R.A.   Lionel Thomas Caswall Rolt (1910-1974).
Technology & Culture. Vol 16(3). July 1975. pp 454-7.
Obituary.

516B GARDNER, Raymond. The man who became a cut figure.
The Guardian. 27 April 1977.
Ostensibly a review of 'Landscape with canals', but more of an appreciation of
Rolt himself.

517 COOMBES, Harry. Man and boat.
Books & Bookmen. Sept 1977. pp 60-1.
Ostensibly a review of 'Landscape with canals', but more of an appreciation of
Rolt's literary work.

517B SHERWEN, Theo. **The Bomford story.** Evesham: Bomford & Evershed,
[1979].
Includes account of Rolt's time with these employers, 1926-8.

518 EMMERSON, George S.   L.T.C. Rolt and the *Great Eastern* affair of
Brunel versus Scott Russell.
Technology & Culture. Vol 21(4). Oct 1980. pp 553-69.
Criticism.of Rolt's interpretation of the relationship between Brunel and Scott
Russell. See Items 519-20.

519 BUCHANAN, R.A. The *Great Eastern* controversy: a comment.
Technology & Culture. Vol 24(1). Jan 1983. pp 98-106.
Defence against Emmerson's criticism in Item 518.

520 EMMERSON, George S. The *Great Eastern* controversy: in response to
Dr. Buchanan.
Technology & Culture. Vol 24(1). Jan 1983. pp 107-13.
See Items 518 19.

521 MACKERSEY, Ian. The last five years.
Waterways World. Vol 13(3). March 1984. pp 36-9; Vol 13(4).
April 1984. pp 40-3; Vol 13(5). May 1984. pp 39-43; and Vol 13(6).
June 1984. pp 48-52.
Four extracts from Item 522.

522 MACKERSEY, Ian. **Tom Rolt and the Cressy years.**
London: Baldwin, 1985. 106pp, illd.
Biographical study of Rolt's canal life, including foundation and early years of
Inland Waterways Association. See also Item 521.
2nd (revd) imp 1991.

523 ROGERSON, Ian, GORDON, Maxim, & ROLT, Sonia. **L.T.C. Rolt: a
bibliography.** Cleobury Mortimer: Baldwin, 1986. 48pp, illd.
2nd edition, revised and extended, 1994.

525 JELLEY, Peter.   L.T.C. Rolt.
Book & Magazine Collector. No 64. July 1989. pp 48-54.
Brief biography and priced bibliography.

527 AWDRY, Rev. W. Adventure of helping to save the railway *in*
CASTELLAN, E. & MASON, P.K. (eds). **Talyllyn 125: a steam
celebration of the world's first preserved railway.** Talyllyn Rly
Preservation Co, 1989. p 3.
In this article, the author reveals 'that I had Tom Rolt in mind when I put the Thin
Controller in charge of the Skarloey Railway.'

529 POTTER, David. **The Talyllyn Railway.** Thomas, 1990.
Chap 3, pp 42-51, 'L.T.C. Rolt'.

531 [CASTELLAN, E.] **Naming of locomotive No. 7 "Tom Rolt". Monday
6th May, 1991. Souvenir brochure.** Talyllyn Rly Co, 1991. [4]pp, illd.

533 CASTELLAN, Eddie. The books of L.T.C. Rolt.
Talyllyn News. No 152. Dec 1991. pp 39-41.

535 ROWLANDS, David. Postscript: a meeting with Tom Rolt.
Ghosts & Scholars. No 11. 1989. p 31.
Postscript to Item 183B; meeting in 1953.

INDEX

References are by Item number. Book titles, shortened where appropriate, are given in SMALL CAPITALS, and periodical titles in *italics*. Illustrations are indicated in **bold**. Books reviewed and titles of articles in periodicals are not indexed.